The AI Whisperer: How Mastering AI Defines Tomorrow's Winners

By Roman Balzan

We stand at the threshold of a new era—one in which the ability to communicate fluently with AI will define who thrives and who struggles. In *The AI Whisperer: How Mastering AI Defines Tomorrow's Winners*, Roman Balzan distills years of hands-on experience and visionary insight into a roadmap for leaders, entrepreneurs, and professionals who refuse to be left behind.

In these pages, you'll discover how to:

- Prompt AI models to transform hours of grunt work into minutes of actionable insight
- Build entire workflows and cultures around AI literacy, amplifying innovation across your organization
- Leverage role-based scenarios and persona frameworks to generate infinite ideas and refine them into practical solutions
- Navigate ethical considerations, ensuring trust, authenticity, and brand integrity guide every decision
- Fuse your personal passion with AI's limitless capacity, turning ordinary efforts into strategic breakthroughs

This isn't another tech trend or a shallow business hack—it's the essential literacy for anyone determined to lead in the age of intelligent machines. If you're ready to outsmart the status quo, set new standards in your field, and make AI your strategic ally, *The AI Whisperer* will show you how to unleash your potential and shape the future.

Copyright © 2024 by Roman Balzan.

All rights reserved.
No part of this publication may be reproduced, distributed, or transmitted in any form or by any means without the prior written permission of the author, except in the case of brief quotations embodied in critical reviews and certain other noncommercial uses permitted by copyright law.

Published by Roman Balzan Publishing, Zurich, Switzerland

ISBN: 9798303027442

While best efforts have been made to ensure the accuracy and completeness of the information contained herein, the author and publisher assume no responsibility for errors, omissions, or contrary interpretation. This book is for informational purposes only and does not constitute professional advice.

Has AI been used in the creation of this work? Yes. AI-assisted drafting and editorial functions were employed in the refinement of textual content.

For inquiries, speaking engagements, or bulk orders, please visit: www.theburnblog.com

First Edition: 2024

Foreword

Throughout my career, I've seen leaders wrestle with change, especially when faced with new technologies. Many cling to outdated methods, while others hesitate, waiting for a clear path forward. *The AI Whisperer* is that path.

This book is more than a guide to prompting AI; it's a framework for rethinking how we work and lead in an era defined by intelligent machines. Rather than fearing automation, this book invites us to embrace augmentation. It transforms AI from a black box into a collaborative ally—one that amplifies our creativity, sharpens our decision-making, and frees us from mundane tasks.

What makes *The AI Whisperer* unique is its focus on mindset. Yes, you'll learn techniques like prompt engineering and persona creation, but you'll also discover how to blend human passion and ethical leadership with AI's power to create something greater than the sum of its parts. This balance of skill and vision makes it a playbook not just for today, but for the future.

As you read, you'll find yourself inspired to lead differently, innovate boldly, and shape the future instead of reacting to it. If you're ready for daily fuel to challenge norms and spark new ideas, I invite you to subscribe to *The Burn Blog* (*www.theburnblog.com*). There, I share bite-sized provocations on leadership, personal growth, AI, and tech—designed to ignite your creativity and keep you ahead of the curve.

The AI Whisperer isn't just a book—it's a catalyst for unlocking the next version of yourself. Let's burn brighter together.

—Roman Balzan

Table of Content

Introduction: The Age of AI Communication ... 5

Chapter 1: From Illiterate to Influencer ... 8

Chapter 2: Navigating the AI Jungle ... 11

Chapter 4: The Language of AI ... 22

Chapter 5: Prompt Engineering 101 ... 31

Chapter 6: Advanced Prompting Techniques ... 40

Chapter 8: Scaling Your Impact with AI ... 58

Chapter 10: The New Skillset ... 74

Chapter 11: Becoming a Cognitive Cyborg ... 83

Chapter 12: Creativity Amplified ... 90

Chapter 13: Leading in the Age of AI ... 98

Chapter 14: Lifelong Learning and Adaptation ... 107

Chapter 15: Overcoming Fear and Resistance ... 110

Conclusion: The Future Belongs to You ... 113

Introduction: The Age of AI Communication

The New Frontier
We're living at a collision point between what we used to know and what we can barely imagine. The old rules of digital proficiency—clicking buttons, crunching spreadsheets, memorizing code—aren't just outdated, they're quaint. The next leap forward isn't about knowing how to use a device; it's about knowing how to talk to one. Welcome to the age of AI communication—where whispering to intelligent machines defines tomorrow's power players.

The Skill That Separates Winners from Irrelevance
In the early days of industry, those who couldn't read and write were left behind. Later, if you couldn't navigate the internet, you faded into irrelevance. Today, if you don't know how to guide artificial intelligence—if you can't shape its responses, harness its reasoning, and push it toward breakthrough insights—you might as well be riding a horse on a highway built for self-driving cars. Let's be crystal clear: The ability to converse fluently with AI isn't a gimmick; it's the new baseline for success.

Why Whispering Matters
When you whisper to AI, you're not just barking commands at a machine. You're forging a partnership with a mind that never sleeps, never tires, and never stops scanning the horizons of possibility. Instead of passing hours on tedious research, you'll compress weeks into minutes. Instead of wrestling with complexity alone, you'll have a patient genius at your beck and call. The way you phrase your prompts can spur the AI to create, strategize, and iterate in ways that give you a decisive edge.

A Personal Revelation
I've watched people go from clueless to unstoppable in a matter of days. I've seen seasoned executives who once wasted hours drafting a quarterly plan now generate razor-sharp strategies in twenty minutes. I've watched innovators harness AI to break down complex challenges—turning vague aspirations into clear action plans that no human consultant could produce so quickly. This isn't theoretical. It's happening, right now.

The High Stakes
Think this is hype? Think again. The marketplace is shifting under your feet. Those who learn to speak AI's language will outmaneuver competitors stuck in old paradigms. They'll make decisions in seconds that others take weeks to consider. They'll leapfrog the slow and the stubborn, staking claims in opportunities most can't even see yet. AI

whispering is the literacy that defines the new era of global influence and innovation.

Your Journey Begins Here
This book is your guide to mastering AI communication. We'll dive deep into why prompting matters, how to hone your technique, and what it takes to become a visionary leader in a world driven by machine intelligence. We'll go beyond theory—showing you the techniques, frameworks, and mental models that transform you from a passive observer into a proactive architect of tomorrow.

Ready? Let's whisper to the future.

Chapter 1: From Illiterate to Influencer—A New Kind of Literacy

The Metaphor That Matters
Picture this: You're standing in a dusty town square at the dawn of the printing press. A few people clutch books, their eyes wide with possibilities. Everyone else? They're illiterate—shut out from the knowledge revolution boiling under the surface. Fast-forward centuries and swap out books for ones and zeros. Digital illiterates got left behind as the world went online. Now, a fresh epoch dawns. The new illiteracy isn't lacking internet skills; it's failing to communicate fluently with artificial intelligence.

Why This Moment Feels Different
We're not talking about a mere upgrade to your productivity apps. This is the difference between horse-drawn carriages and jets. Between hand-cranked calculations and quantum leaps of reasoning. AI can tear down walls—market barriers, language barriers, even mental roadblocks—and rewrite entire industries overnight. But only if you know how to talk to it.

The Price of Falling Behind
Everyone loves to think they can dodge a revolution. "I don't need that skill," they say. "I'll manage just fine." Sure—until your competitor deploys an AI ally to design, test, and launch products in a fraction of the time you need just to brainstorm. Until investors start asking you, "Why are you still doing everything the slow way?" Until talent flocks to teams that leverage AI's infinite capacity for insight, leaving you in a talent drought you never saw coming.

A Shifting Landscape
Remember when typing was a niche skill? Or when social media was a teenager's toy? Those who treated these shifts seriously gained an unfair advantage. Now, prompting AI—crafting powerful instructions that yield brilliant outputs—is the new secret weapon. If you master it, you don't just keep up, you catapult ahead.

From Chaos to Clarity
Embrace this shift, and you'll find something curious happens. It's not just about AI producing brilliant work. It's about you learning to think, plan, and communicate with more structure and clarity. As you refine your prompts, you refine your own mind. You go from a jumble of half-baked ideas to crisp strategies that inspire action. The machine's logic rubs off on you, sharpening your mental edge.

Crossing the Threshold

The first step is acknowledging that prompt engineering—a skill that, just a few years ago, didn't even exist—is now essential. Instead of lamenting that change, seize it. Recognize that you're walking through a doorway that separates yesterday's thinkers from tomorrow's architects of possibility. The threshold is here, and on the other side awaits speed, sophistication, and solutions you never thought possible.

Chapter 2: Navigating the AI Jungle—Tools, Models, and Opportunity

A New, Uncharted Wilderness
Imagine you've been dropped into the heart of an unexplored jungle. Dense foliage stretches in every direction, teeming with hidden resources and lurking pitfalls. That's the AI ecosystem today. New models appear monthly, even weekly. One moment, a language model sets the world on fire; the next, an image generator steals the spotlight. Keeping up can feel impossible. Yet, in these untamed lands lie the seeds of tomorrow's empires—if you know where to dig.

The Beating Heart: Large Language Models
Large Language Models (LLMs) are your machete, compass, and guide rolled into one. They're the core technology that transforms raw data into coherent strategies, stories, and insights. With a well-crafted prompt, an LLM can map markets, draft proposals, brainstorm ad campaigns, or summarize complex legal briefs in seconds. But wielding them carelessly is like swinging a machete in the dark—you'll end up with nonsense or, worse, misdirections. To

thrive, you must learn how to direct these models like a seasoned explorer charting unknown terrain.

Beyond Text: The Expanding Arsenal
LLMs are the start, not the end. Voice synthesis tools can make your brand's messaging more personal and immediate. Image generators bring visuals to life at zero hour. Code assistants translate your vague product ideas into functioning prototypes overnight. Specialized domain models—financial analysts, medical advisors, compliance watchdogs—stand ready to feed you niche insights with surgical precision. This is a world where every problem can be attacked from multiple angles, where every angle has its tool, and every tool bends to your prompting prowess.

The Perils of the Shiny Object
In a landscape of endless new releases, it's tempting to chase every shiny object. Don't. Hype without strategy is a one-way ticket to disappointment. The winners aren't those who hoard tools, but those who deploy the right ones at the right time with surgical focus. Mastery means understanding each tool's strengths and weaknesses, then orchestrating them into a symphony of intelligence that delivers exactly what you need, when you need it.

Integration: The Hidden Superpower
Real power emerges when you integrate multiple AIs into cohesive workflows. Imagine this: a voice assistant records

your brainstormed instructions, transcribes them into text, which a language model refines into a strategic plan. Another model turns that plan into a polished pitch deck, while a domain-specific AI checks for compliance and cultural nuances. Instead of patchwork solutions, you get seamless workflows that shrink timelines from weeks to hours. Integration makes you unstoppable.

A Landscape Still in Flux
Here's the wild part: we're early in this revolution. Tools evolve by the month, capabilities surge by the quarter, and entire categories of AI appear almost overnight. This is fertile ground for the brave and forward-thinking. If you embrace the chaos—learn to navigate it, stay curious, test relentlessly—you'll stand on the cutting edge of an era that leaves the timid behind.

Opportunity in the Shadows
Consider this chapter a map shoved into your hands as you take your first steps into the AI jungle. It can't detail every path or warn you of every trap. But it should inspire you to move boldly, to see confusion not as an obstacle but as a sign of undiscovered gold. In a world where everyone else is intimidated or overwhelmed, you will remain calm, strategic, and hungry.

Because in this new wilderness, the fearless, prepared, and adaptive won't just survive—they'll conquer.

Chapter 3: Burning the Old Myths to the Ground—And Building a New Mindset

Torching the Lies That Hold You Back
Change unsettles us. The arrival of AI as a strategic partner, a thinking companion, and a creative co-pilot ruffles feathers at every level—executives, analysts, entrepreneurs, freelancers. Whenever we face a new power, clinging to old myths feels safer than forging new paths. But safety is an illusion. Today's myths don't just mislead; they lock you out of a future where success isn't about who you know or how hard you grind, but how fluently you whisper to intelligent machines.

We're going to name these myths, set them on fire, and warm our hands over the blaze. Because once these mental obstacles are ash, you'll see how far and how fast you can go.

Myth #1: "AI Will Steal My Job"
This is the big one, right? The monster under every

professional's bed. The truth is simpler and more dynamic: AI will shape-shift your job. The dull, mechanical tasks you hate—compiling endless reports, sifting through data, drafting the same memo for the hundredth time—those vanish. In their place, you gain bandwidth for strategic creativity, for charting futures no one's yet envisioned.

Think of when the printing press arrived. Did storytellers vanish? No, they gained access to bigger audiences. The internet didn't destroy commerce; it multiplied it a thousandfold. AI isn't an eraser; it's a multiplier. If you learn to prompt and steer AI, you're not replaced—you're upgraded. You become a conductor in an era of symphonic intelligence. Refuse, and yes, you might find yourself playing the same old tune while the world's moved on to orchestras flying through digital skies.

Myth #2: "I Need to Be a Tech Genius"
Many imagine prompting AI as a superpower reserved for coders and data scientists. That's yesterday's story. Prompting isn't about code; it's about clarity, context, and communication. If you can explain a concept to a friend, you can prompt an AI. The technical barrier is ankle-high, not sky-high.

Remember the voice-driven workflows we discussed? You speak naturally—just talk as if explaining your challenge to a colleague. The AI transcribes your words, and then you refine and feed them to the model. It's more like having a conversation than writing code. You say, "I need a product roadmap for Q1," or "Here are four growth pillars; help me integrate them into a budget framework." No PhD required—just the willingness to organize your thoughts and hit "enter."

And here's the twist: this practice makes you sharper. As you learn to prompt effectively, you refine your own thinking. You become a better strategist, a more incisive communicator. The AI becomes your mental gym partner, spotting you as you lift heavier conceptual weights.

Myth #3: "AI Is Always Right"
Oh, how we wish for a perfect oracle. AI models can be brilliant, but they're also flawed. They can produce "hallucinations"—confident nonsense dressed up in eloquent phrases. They can be biased, confused, or plain wrong. Believing they're infallible is like thinking every charismatic speaker must be telling the truth.

Your role here is curator, critic, editor. You prompt, the AI responds, and you judge. You might ask the model to explain its reasoning step-by-step (Chain-of-Thought prompting), compare multiple solutions (self-consistency checks), or adopt a persona that challenges its own assumptions. The myth that AI is always right crumbles when you realize your value doesn't vanish in an AI-driven world—it intensifies. Your human judgment remains the gold standard.

Myth #4: "Prompting Is Just a Side Skill"
Still think prompting is a cute party trick? Consider the difference between an amateur who tosses random queries at an AI and a skilled prompter who orchestrates entire workflows. The amateur gets generic, often shallow answers. The prompter unlocks a cascade of strategic insights, aligning them with brand voice, market constraints, and upcoming deadlines. The amateur struggles; the prompter soars.

Remember how we discussed custom personas—like "The Conciliere," a persona you define to produce punchy, provocative thought-leadership posts with a Godfather-esque tone? Or the Swiss Finance Compliance Expert persona that ensures every piece of marketing advice you get aligns with FINMA and DPA rules? That's not a trivial add-on; it's a transformative skill. You're not just asking for help; you're crafting a digital expert who speaks your language, understands your constraints, and amplifies your capabilities.

Prompting is power. Belittle it, and you leave untapped potential on the table.

Myth #5: "It's Too Late to Start"
We're at the dawn, not dusk, of this revolution. Early internet adopters weren't always geniuses; they were simply bold. They jumped in before everything was mapped, monetized, and monopolized. That's where we stand now with AI prompting.

The skills are still rare. The territory is still uncharted. By learning now, you position yourself as a pioneer, someone who can shape best practices rather than follow them. You're not chasing a train that left the station; you're boarding it as it's being built.

Myth #6: "Only Written Prompts Matter"
You might think prompting means typing paragraphs all day. Not necessarily. Voice interaction—a theme we've touched on—is a game-changer. Talking to your AI as if it's a trusted colleague, then refining that transcript and feeding it back into the model, turns your spoken insight into strategic output. This voice-first approach lets you brainstorm, instruct, and iterate at lightning speed. It frees you from your keyboard and brings you closer to a human-like collaboration with your digital ally.

The myth that it's all about written text dissolves when you see how seamlessly your spoken intentions become tangible strategies. By embracing voice, you multiply your cognitive bandwidth, letting your natural speech patterns guide the AI. Over time, you learn to speak more coherently and strategically, evolving your very thought process.

Myth #7: "AI Undermines Authentic Human Creativity"
Some fear that using AI means losing personal creativity. In reality, AI can be a creativity amplifier. Suppose you're stuck on a narrative twist for your marketing campaign or searching for fresh angles on user engagement. By prompting the AI—"Generate three unorthodox ideas based on our brand voice and user surveys"—you spark a

loop of inspiration. The machine serves up possibilities you hadn't considered, and you refine, combine, or reject them until you forge something uniquely yours.

Your authenticity doesn't vanish; it becomes sharper. AI acts as a catalyst, not a replacement. The myth that creativity erodes under machine guidance falls away when you realize you still hold the final call. Your taste, your moral compass, your aesthetic sense remain intact. AI just gives you more raw material to sculpt.

Burning the Myths, Forging New Capabilities
These myths want you timid, hesitant, clinging to old patterns. But you're here to pioneer, not preserve. By incinerating these lies, you reveal the rich soil beneath. In this fertile ground, your newfound prompt skills will sprout into a garden of capabilities—rapid problem-solving, nuanced strategy development, persona-driven content creation, instant compliance checks, and performance reviews that practically write themselves.

The myths are ash now. Good riddance. Step beyond their smoldering remains and embrace the reality: AI prompting is your competitive edge, your personal growth driver, and your strategic amplifier. You're not losing control; you're gaining leverage. You're not being replaced; you're being elevated.

So, say goodbye to fear and uncertainty. Say hello to a world where your next prompt might define your next breakthrough.

Chapter 4: The Language of AI—Why Prompts Matter

Speaking a New Tongue

Every era invents a new vocabulary that sets its winners apart. The printing press demanded literacy. The internet demanded digital fluency. Now, AI ushers in a language where your words shape not just how information is retrieved, but how intelligence itself is generated. Mastering prompts is learning to speak a new tongue—a language less about grammar and syntax, more about clarity, context, and intent. Instead of merely retrieving facts, you summon insights, craft strategies, and orchestrate entire workflows. Welcome to the world where words create leverage.

From Static Queries to Active Dialogues

In the old paradigm, you typed questions into a search bar and hit "Enter," hoping for something relevant. With AI-driven prompting, you're no longer fishing blindly in a data ocean. You're having a conversation with a mind that can reason (albeit in its own pattern-based way), iterate, and learn from your cues.

Consider how voice interfaces amplify this shift. Instead of fumbling with keywords, you speak: "I'm planning next quarter's product launch. Here's what I know…" You relay background details, constraints, and targets as if briefing a new team member. The AI listens, transcribes, and turns your spoken complexity into structured clarity. Then, with a refined prompt—perhaps more context or a role assignment—you push it further, delving into scenarios, fleshing out milestones, and extracting marketing hooks. You're not making queries; you're shaping an ongoing dialogue that evolves as your ideas refine.

Why the Right Prompt Transcends the Wrong One
Imagine two professionals tackling the same task. The first says, "Give me a marketing plan." The AI responds with a generic template—nothing special. The second says, "You are my marketing strategist. Considering our four growth pillars (X, Y, Z, and W) and the KPIs I provided (conversion rates, retention, and brand awareness), craft a three-month organic social media plan focusing on LinkedIn and Instagram. Align it with our ethical compliance rules from FINMA and DPA. Present it in bullet points, including deadlines and expected outcomes."

Guess who gets a useful answer?

The second professional's prompt is a masterstroke of clarity, context, and constraints. It's role-based, offering the AI a persona to inhabit ("my marketing strategist"). It references known constraints (compliance rules). It specifies outputs (bullet points, deadlines, expected outcomes). The AI doesn't guess what you want; it knows. This is the heart of prompt design—transforming vague requests into laser-targeted commands that yield actionable brilliance.

The DNA of a Good Prompt
What makes a prompt sing? A few key elements:

1. **Context:** Instead of throwing the AI into the dark, you turn on the lights. You mention your industry, goals, and limitations.

2. **Clarity:** No ambiguous requests. If you need a 500-word summary, say so. If you want three separate options, specify. If you prefer a certain tone or style, tell the model explicitly.

3. **Constraints:** Boundaries sharpen the AI's focus. A time frame, a budget cap, a target audience—every constraint refines the AI's internal logic, driving it toward the exact solution you need.

4. **Purpose:** Explain the "why." When the AI understands the ultimate goal—educating a new audience, streamlining a workflow, impressing

investors—it can shape its response more strategically.

5. **Role Assignments:** Give the AI a persona or perspective. "Act as a seasoned CFO" or "You are my chief marketing officer." This triggers the model to adopt a voice and reasoning style that suits your scenario.

By weaving these elements together, you stop talking at the AI and start conversing with it. You become an architect of intelligence, drafting blueprints for the machine to follow.

Iterative Refinement—The Conversation Continues
Think prompting is a one-shot deal? Far from it. The first response you get is often a rough draft. Use that draft as a stepping stone. Ask the AI to clarify its reasoning, to provide examples, to challenge its own assumptions. If the output misses a detail, prompt again with more specifics. If it's too complex, ask it to simplify. Over time, this back-and-forth polishes rough stones into gems.

For instance, say you asked the AI for a product roadmap and got something decent but not stunning. Now you prompt: "Explain why you chose these milestones and how each contributes to our Q1 revenue goals. Also, list potential pitfalls and suggest mitigations." With each request, you sharpen the AI's understanding of your needs, and it refines its answers accordingly.

Voice-Driven Improvements—Your Brain on Display
When you rely on voice prompts, an interesting phenomenon occurs: you start structuring your thoughts before you speak. You think, "What's my ultimate goal here? Which details does the AI need?" Over time, your mental organization improves. You become a more strategic thinker by necessity. The act of formulating a precise prompt—whether spoken or typed—makes your own reasoning clearer.

This personal growth loop is invaluable. The more you refine your prompts, the sharper your thinking, and the more valuable the AI's outputs become. It's a virtuous cycle: better prompts, better insights, smarter you.

Role-Based Personas—Sculpting AI into Your Dream Team
We touched on persona creation before. Let's go deeper. By defining roles, you mold the AI's "personality." Want a gritty, no-nonsense strategist like "The Conciliere"? You can instruct the AI to adopt a tone, style, and worldview that push your thinking into bold territory. Need a compliance guru who ensures every marketing idea aligns with Swiss regulations? Prompt the AI to act as a "Swiss

Finance Compliance Expert." Suddenly, it's reviewing proposals with a hawk's eye for rules and restrictions.

These personas aren't gimmicks—they're powerful tools. They allow you to tap into different viewpoints, shifting the AI's output from generalist to specialist, from vague to crystal-clear. It's like having a lineup of experts on speed dial, ready to dissect your challenges from multiple angles.

Guiding the AI's Thought Process with Chain-of-Thought
Some problems demand step-by-step reasoning. Enter Chain-of-Thought prompting. By asking the AI to reveal its reasoning process before giving the final answer, you can verify its logic, correct errors mid-stream, and ensure the solution is sound.

Picture this scenario: "List the steps you took to arrive at this conclusion, and show me each decision point." The AI then breaks down its mental journey, revealing where it found data, how it weighed options, and why it chose a certain path. If something looks off, you refine the prompt or ask it to reconsider. This transparency transforms the AI from a black box into a glasshouse, where you can watch the reasoning unfold.

Self-Consistency and Multiple Perspectives
What if you're not sure what approach to take? Ask the AI

for multiple solutions, each with a different angle. Then prompt it again to pick the most consistent or logical one. This is how you transform a single AI into a panel of advisers. You're not stuck with one viewpoint; you orchestrate a debate and then pick the winner. It's intellectual arbitrage—your prompts orchestrating a chorus of ideas.

Physical vs. Digital Literacy—A New Mind-Body Connection
We're taught to articulate ourselves in writing and speech. Prompting AI adds a new dimension. You now articulate yourself in a form that's instantly actionable, a language that doesn't just convey meaning but executes complex tasks. This evolution mirrors physical literacy (like learning to dance or play an instrument) except your "instrument" is an AI's cognitive engine. You refine your "moves" (prompts), achieve certain "techniques" (chain-of-thought, personas, constraints), and over time, gain mastery.

Your Competitive Edge—Why Prompting Matters More Than Ever
In a hyper-competitive environment, everyone fights for small advantages. Prompt mastery isn't a small advantage; it's a strategic arsenal. With it, you can produce marketing plans in minutes, run compliance checks instantly, brainstorm a dozen product concepts by lunch, and finalize

a roadmap by dinner. Without it, you watch competitors run circles around you.

Seeding Your Future with Each Prompt
Every prompt you craft is an investment in your future workflow. As you discover what works best—certain keywords, specific structures, favorite personas—you build a library of templates that become your secret weapons. Over time, you won't just be prompting off-the-cuff; you'll have a "prompt portfolio" to draw upon, accelerating every new initiative. Your prompts become intellectual capital you can deploy at will.

The Art and Science of Prompting
Think of prompting as both art and science. The science lies in understanding the mechanics—context, constraints, chain-of-thought, iteration. The art emerges when you blend these elements gracefully, crafting prompts that resonate with your goals and style. No two prompters produce identical results. Your unique voice, priorities, and methodologies shape how the AI responds.

This chapter is your primer in the language of AI. By understanding why prompts matter and how to design them masterfully, you set the stage for everything that follows. In the chapters ahead, we'll explore more advanced techniques, integrate prompting across entire organizations, and refine the cultural and ethical frameworks that guide responsible AI usage.

But for now, know this: mastering the language of prompts isn't optional. It's the gateway to a future where your words don't just describe reality—they help create it.

Chapter 5: Prompt Engineering 101—Your Blueprint for Consistent Brilliance

From Inspiration to Implementation
You know prompting matters. You've felt the gravity of its potential. But knowing isn't enough—you need a toolkit. You need to translate big ideas into daily practice. That's what Prompt Engineering 101 is all about: taking the abstract art of asking the right question and turning it into a reliable, repeatable process. This chapter is your blueprint, your starter pack for ensuring every prompt you craft edges you closer to strategic brilliance.

The Prompt Lifecycle—From Rough Draft to Refined Gem
Effective prompting isn't a one-off event; it's a cycle. You start with a rough idea, you test it, and you refine. Over time, you develop a sixth sense for what works. Consider this lifecycle:

1. **Ideation:** You have a need—maybe it's a marketing plan, a product feature list, or a compliance check.

Your first prompt is a guess, a rough sketch of what you want.

2. **First Draft:** You get an initial output. Maybe it's underwhelming, vague, or too long. That's expected.

3. **Refinement:** Based on the response, you add details, constraints, and context to your prompt. You clarify your goals or specify a format.

4. **Validation:** You evaluate the new output. Better? Good. If still not perfect, refine again.

5. **Repeat and Archive:** Once you land on something extraordinary, you save that prompt structure in your personal library. It's now a template you can reuse, adapt, and repurpose.

Over time, your prompt portfolio grows into a treasure chest of proven structures. The more you prompt, the faster you find the sweet spot. Iteration leads to mastery.

Five Key Techniques for Prompt Mastery

1. **Command, Don't Beg:**
Instead of "Could you maybe give me some ideas?"

say "List five actionable growth strategies." Be direct. The AI thrives on clarity and assertiveness. A confident voice sets the stage for confident outputs.

2. **Use Examples Generously**:
   If you want a certain style, show a sample. "Here is an example of the tone and structure I like…" If you want a specific format—say a bullet-point list with deadlines—provide a mini template. Examples act like training wheels for the AI, guiding it toward your target result.

3. **Context Is King (Again)**:
   Don't assume the AI remembers what you said 10 prompts ago. Reiterate crucial details. "As a reminder, our Q1 goal is a 20% revenue increase in the U.S. market." Stack context in every prompt so the AI never flies blind.

4. **Time, Format, and Length Constraints**:
   Want a short summary? Say "Explain in 200 words." Need a breakdown by month? Say "Provide a three-month roadmap with one milestone per month." Constraints transform open-ended tasks into laser-focused outputs.

5. **Add Roles and Personas Liberally:**
   "You are my CFO—evaluate the financial feasibility of this plan." "Act as a brand strategist—refine this messaging." Roles tap into the AI's ability to adapt tone, perspective, and priorities, yielding outputs tailored to your needs.

The Power of Chain-of-Thought and Iterative Drilling
When complexity abounds, break it down. Instead of demanding a final solution upfront, ask the AI to show its reasoning steps. For example:

- "Explain step-by-step how you arrived at these three marketing tactics, considering budget constraints and brand voice."

- If a step seems off, drill deeper: "Why did you assume a $10,000 monthly ad spend? Reconsider this with a $5,000 limit."

This iterative drilling isn't just about getting the right answer; it's about understanding the logic behind it. You're training both the model and yourself—learning which prompts lead to optimal reasoning paths.

Use the Voice Interface as a Prompt Pre-Processor
When you talk through your problem before writing it down, you're essentially brainstorming out loud. Try this:

- Speak into a voice note: "I need a marketing campaign for our new eco-friendly product. It targets millennials who value sustainability, and I have a budget of $10,000 for Q2."

- Listen to your own explanation. Is it clear? Missing details? By the time you type the prompt, you've already clarified your thoughts. This pre-processing step ensures your typed prompt hits the ground running.

Building Your Prompt Library—Your Personal Arsenal
Every time you refine a prompt until it sings, store it. Categorize them by function—marketing plans, compliance checks, persona assignments, product roadmaps. Over time, you become faster, pulling from a rich repertoire of tried-and-true templates. This library turns you from a beginner feeling your way in the dark into a veteran who lights up every challenge at first try.

For instance, a template might look like this:

- **Situation:** "We're launching a B2B SaaS tool next quarter."

- **Role Prompt:** "Act as a seasoned B2B product marketing manager."

- **Constraints:** "Budget: $5,000. Timeline: 3 months. Market: Financial advisors in Switzerland."

- **Format:** "Provide a 4-step action plan, each step with a monthly milestone and measurable outcome."

- **Persona Inputs:** "Incorporate FINMA and DPA compliance considerations where relevant."

With this template in hand, next time you face a similar challenge, you just fill in the blanks, maybe tweak the timeline or audience, and you're off.

Experimentation and A/B Testing Prompts

Don't assume your first good prompt is the best prompt. Try slight variations and compare results. Maybe giving more context upfront yields richer details. Maybe shortening your request leads to sharper outputs. Treat prompts like hypotheses—test, measure, refine. Over time, you'll internalize what works best, reducing the guesswork and increasing your hit rate.

From Functional to Inspirational
Prompts aren't just orders. They can inspire. You can say, "Give me three innovative but ethically sound manipulation tactics for negotiating contracts, in the voice of a stoic philosopher." The AI might produce a bizarre blend of strategic advice and timeless wisdom—something you'd never have thought of yourself. Creative prompting unlocks not just efficiency but imagination. The world opens up as you realize prompts can spark unexpected insights.

Performance Reviews, Compliance Checks, and Creativity Boosts
Let's get concrete:

- **Performance Reviews:**
  "Act as my HR advisor. Given these employee KPIs and qualitative feedback, draft a balanced performance review in a professional, encouraging tone. Include one constructive criticism and two actionable growth steps."

- **Compliance Checks:**
  "You are a Swiss Finance Compliance Expert.

Review the following marketing copy and identify any potential FINMA or DPA violations. Suggest revisions that maintain impact but ensure full compliance."

- **Creativity Boosts:**
  "You are my creative muse. I have a storyline about a fintech startup founder facing market skepticism. Suggest three plot twists that heighten tension, build empathy, and lead to a triumphant resolution."

See how each scenario is shaped by context, roles, constraints, and a clear purpose? These examples transform general tasks into laser-focused prompts that deliver actionable results.

Your Path to Mastery
Prompt Engineering 101 isn't about perfection on your first try. It's about understanding the process, embracing iteration, and seeing prompts as flexible tools rather than rigid commands. With each experiment, you carve away uncertainty. With each refined prompt, you become a sharper thinker, communicator, and strategist.

Eventually, you won't even realize you're "prompting" an AI. You'll just be working—rapidly, efficiently, creatively—using a skill so integrated it feels as natural as conversation.

Except these conversations produce insights, solutions, and strategies at scale and speed humans alone can't match.

That's the essence of prompt engineering. It's your gateway to a world where well-structured words unlock unprecedented capabilities. Embrace the journey, and watch as your workflows transform, your thinking sharpens, and your influence expands.

Chapter 6: Advanced Prompting Techniques—Crafting a Higher Order of Intelligence

Beyond Basics—Becoming a Prompt Virtuoso

By now, you're not just dabbling with AI—you're orchestrating it. You've learned to set context, define roles, and iterate prompts until they sing. But advanced prompting isn't about playing by the rules; it's about bending them in your favor. It's about turning a single AI into an army of specialized thinkers, each refining your ideas, challenging assumptions, and pushing your strategy toward higher ground.

This chapter takes you past the fundamentals into the domain of virtuosity. We'll explore meta-techniques—prompt chaining, multi-role interplay, scenario simulation, chain-of-thought reasoning, and self-consistency checks—that help you sculpt the AI's cognitive processes like a master craftsman shaping marble.

Role-Playing and Scenario Setting: Your Private Theater of Minds

Sometimes, you need more than a single "voice" advising you. You crave the richness of multiple perspectives—like assembling a council of experts in your head. Advanced prompting lets you build this council from scratch. Consider these techniques:

- **Role-Stacking:** You can layer roles within a single prompt: "Act first as a Chief Marketing Officer, propose a strategy. Then, as a Compliance Officer, critique it. Finally, as a Product Manager, refine the combined output into a workable roadmap." With one prompt, you orchestrate a dialogue among virtual minds, capturing the complexity of real-world decision-making.

- **Scenario Simulations:** Instead of asking for static answers, invite the AI into dynamic scenarios. "Imagine we're facing a sudden market downturn. You are my strategic think tank—outline two possible responses and their consequences." Or even: "We've just gained unexpected funding. As a panel of experts (economist, brand strategist, operations guru), debate the best use of these resources." Scenario setting transforms sterile Q&A into living narratives that reveal blind spots and uncover hidden opportunities.

Chain-of-Thought Prompting: Watching the AI Think Out Loud

When the path to a solution isn't straightforward, chain-of-thought prompting lets you see the model's reasoning steps. Instead of a final answer dropping from the sky, you prompt the AI to show its work. For example:

- "Explain each step of your reasoning as you determine the best marketing channel for our new product, starting with problem definition, moving through data analysis, and concluding with your chosen channel. Then give the final recommendation."

This technique reveals the machine's internal logic. If something feels off, you can intercept and correct it mid-stream. It's like reading the AI's mind—transforming it from a black box into a transparent partner you can shape in real time.

Self-Consistency and Multiple Perspectives: Building a Brain Trust Inside the Machine

Why settle for one reasoning chain when you can have several? Self-consistency techniques ask the AI to consider multiple angles, produce different solution paths, and then reconcile them. For instance:

- "Generate three distinct plans, each based on different assumptions. Then evaluate which plan is the most consistent with our brand's long-term vision and why."

By forcing the AI to debate with itself, you simulate a mini-think tank. You're no longer limited to a single perspective; you're harnessing parallel universes of thought and merging them into a stronger final solution. This approach builds resilience into your decision-making process, ensuring that the final outcome has passed multiple internal tests.

Tree-of-Thoughts: Branching Intelligence
If chain-of-thought is a linear reasoning path, tree-of-thought takes it exponential. Instead of one chain, you prompt the AI to branch out at decision points, exploring multiple futures. For example:

- "At each step of designing our user onboarding flow, propose two divergent options, analyze their pros and cons, and choose one to continue forward until we reach a final design."

Tree-of-thought prompts simulate exploration at scale. You're no longer walking a single path through the forest; you're surveying multiple trails simultaneously and choosing the best route. This iterative branching mimics how expert strategists consider parallel options before locking in.

Chaining Prompts Together—From Idea to Execution
Sometimes one prompt isn't enough. You can chain prompts so each output becomes the input for the next, creating a pipeline of intelligence:

1. **Initial Brainstorm:** "List ten innovative growth tactics for our FinTech startup."

2. **Filtering:** "From those ten, select the three most feasible given a $20,000 budget and strict FINMA compliance."

3. **Detailed Planning:** "For each of those three, provide a 30-day action plan with weekly milestones."

4. **Risk Assessment:** "Now, as a compliance officer, identify potential pitfalls in each plan and suggest adjustments."

By chaining prompts, you break complex goals into stages. Each step refines the previous output, layering context and complexity until you arrive at a highly polished result. It's like running a relay race where you hand off the baton to specialized AI modes, each contributing their expertise.

The Power of Personas Revisited—Summoning Allies on Demand

We've discussed personas like "The Conciliere" before. Now imagine an entire cast of personas you can summon at will. Need bold strategic insights? Call forth The Conciliere. Need a compliance lens? Introduce the Swiss Finance Compliance Expert. Want a performance review assistant that elegantly balances praise and constructive feedback? Invoke "Perf Bot."

Combine them: "First, The Conciliere provides a raw, unapologetic strategic idea. Then Perf Bot refines it into a team-friendly implementation plan. Finally, the Compliance Expert ensures it's fully above board." You're not just prompting AI; you're directing a play starring characters you invented, each with their own strengths and specialties.

Voice Interaction: A Real-Time Negotiation with Intelligence

Think of advanced prompting as a conversation, not just a command line. Using voice, you can negotiate with the AI in real-time. You say, "Break down that last idea further," and instantly the AI presents a more granular analysis. You respond, "Now challenge that assumption," and it does so.

This dynamic interplay, aided by voice, turns AI consultation into a fluid, iterative dialogue. Instead of carefully crafting a perfect prompt upfront, you co-create solutions on the fly.

Over time, you might find yourself thinking in a more structured, strategic manner because you know you can ask the AI to pivot, elaborate, or reassess at any moment. Your mindset shifts from linear query to improvisational jam session with a band of virtual experts.

Integration with External Data and Tools
Advanced prompters also learn to integrate external data sources. Maybe you feed the AI a table of monthly revenue data or a snippet of market research. You say, "Analyze this data and highlight the top three growth levers," then build on that output with scenario prompts, persona checks, and compliance reviews. By blending raw facts with insightful personas and reasoning frameworks, you create a knowledge machine that's both deeply informed and strikingly flexible.

Ethical and Cultural Dimensions of Advanced Prompting
As you master these techniques, remember that with great power comes responsibility. Chain-of-thought reasoning, persona-driven advice, and scenario simulations can steer decisions in profound ways. Ensure your values and ethics guide the process. If you're simulating manipulative tactics,

frame them as thought experiments aimed at understanding influence—not as malicious blueprints. If you're tackling compliance, respect those rules genuinely. AI is a tool, but you hold the moral compass.

Honing Your Craft Through Continuous Practice
Like any art, advanced prompting thrives on repetition, curiosity, and reflection. Try new personas. Experiment with chain-of-thought on different tasks—budget planning, narrative building, investment strategies. Request multiple perspectives, then ask the AI to judge its own consistency. The more you push the boundaries, the more you'll discover unexpected synergies.

Soon, you'll find yourself orchestrating complex strategic sessions—ideation, refinement, risk assessment, compliance check, final polish—all through a series of elegantly chained prompts. You'll feel like a general commanding an army of brilliant, tireless advisors.

Your Journey to Prompting Mastery
At this stage, you're no longer just "using AI." You're crafting a multi-dimensional intelligence ecosystem where each prompt is a carefully chosen note in a grand symphony of thinking. The techniques in this chapter aren't gimmicks; they're accelerators. They multiply your reach, giving you depth, breadth, and agility.

In the chapters to come, we'll move beyond individual mastery to scaling these skills across teams, organizations, and entire industries. But for now, revel in the knowledge that you're stepping into a new dimension of capability. Through advanced prompting, you're building a second brain—one that can reason, debate, explore, and refine. You're not just whispering to AI; you're conducting it, and the music you create together can change everything.

Chapter 7: Turning Ideas into Action—Real-World Case Studies

From Theory to High-Stakes Reality
You've sharpened your skills, learned to whisper, orchestrate, and challenge the AI's reasoning. You've crafted personas and scenarios, refined your prompts, and glimpsed the extraordinary potential at your fingertips. But what does all this look like in the real world? How do you step out of the classroom and onto the battlefield—where market shifts, compliance regulations, investor expectations, and human emotions collide?

This chapter is about making it all tangible. We'll dissect real scenarios—marketing campaigns, product roadmaps, performance evaluations, compliance checks—and show you exactly how to deploy your prompting superpowers in the heat of the moment.

Scenario 1: Launching a Bold New Marketing Strategy
Picture this: You're CMO of a mid-stage fintech startup. You're aiming for a high-impact campaign that boosts brand awareness, resonates with ethically-driven millennials, and adheres to Swiss FINMA regulations. You

need to break through the noise—fast, with limited budget. Yesterday's methods—guessing, endless brainstorming, and clunky spreadsheets—won't cut it.

- **Initial Prompt:**
  "You are my Chief Marketing Officer. Our fintech product targets Swiss millennials who value transparency and ethical investment. I have a $10,000 monthly budget and need a 3-month content strategy on LinkedIn and Instagram. Drive brand awareness while respecting FINMA guidelines and encourage ethical decision-making."

- **Refinement:**
  The AI spits out a decent plan, but it feels generic. Time to chain prompts:
  "As a Swiss Finance Compliance Expert, review the above plan. Identify any FINMA or DPA compliance risks. Suggest revisions that keep it impactful but ensure full compliance."

- **Persona Interplay:**
  Now you have a compliance-filtered version. Next, call on The Conciliere persona for a bolder, more provocative angle.
  "As The Conciliere, spice up our messaging with a darker, more provocative tone—still ethical and respectful, but capturing immediate attention. Then

integrate these tweaks back into the compliant version of the plan."

- **Chain-of-Thought Reasoning:**
  "Explain your reasoning step-by-step: why these platforms, why these particular influencers, and how each tactic aligns with our brand's ethical stance. Show me your logic before finalizing the strategy."

The result? A marketing plan forged in minutes—rich, compliant, bold, and precisely tailored. Instead of weeks of human back-and-forth, you orchestrated multiple perspectives in a single afternoon.

Scenario 2: Engineering a Product Roadmap with Multiple Stakeholders

You've got a new SaaS tool to launch next quarter. Engineers scream for more development time; sales demands immediate features; customers crave a better onboarding flow. It's chaos—unless you use prompts to transform it into a symphony.

- **Initial Prompt:**
  "You are my Product Manager. Given our backlog of 20 features, a 3-month timeline, and a team of 5 developers, prioritize which features to build first.

Our goal: improve user retention by 15% and reduce onboarding friction by 30%."

- **Chaining Prompts for Perspective:**
  First, get the AI's top picks. Next, introduce another prompt:
  "Now act as a Senior Engineer. From the chosen features, identify technical constraints, estimate dev time, and suggest any trade-offs."
  Then, chain again:
  "As a Customer Success Manager, review these features from a user delight perspective. Are we missing something crucial?"
  Finally, integrate:
  "Combine insights from Product Manager, Engineer, and Customer Success perspectives. Resolve conflicts and produce a final roadmap that balances feasibility, user impact, and strategic goals."

The AI now produces a composite roadmap influenced by multiple roles—just like a real leadership team huddled in a conference room. Except this meeting never ends; you can keep iterating until perfection emerges.

Scenario 3: Performance Reviews That Actually Help People Grow

Performance reviews can be awkward, tedious, and biased.

With prompting, you transform them into constructive, empathetic, and actionable dialogues.

- **Initial Prompt:**
  "You are my HR Advisor. Given these employee KPIs (X, Y, Z), and qualitative feedback (A, B, C), draft a performance review that balances praise with one area of improvement. The tone should be professional, encouraging, and empathetic."

- **Refinement Through Roles:**
  If you sense the review is too generic, ask:
  "Adopt the persona of a leadership coach who values personal growth. Suggest 2-3 career development actions that align with the employee's skill set and company goals."
  Then get a second opinion:
  "As a Diversity & Inclusion Officer, ensure the language is inclusive, free of bias, and acknowledges the employee's cultural background. Suggest improvements."

After a few iterations, you'll have a performance review that's fair, motivating, culturally sensitive, and growth-oriented. No more last-minute scribbles or vague feedback. It's a polished, meaningful document that employee and manager alike will appreciate.

Scenario 4: Compliance Checks in a Tight Regulatory Environment

Imagine you're drafting messaging for a financial product. One slip and you risk regulatory scrutiny. Manually triple-checking every word is painful. Instead, prompt the AI:

- **Initial Prompt:**
  "You are a Swiss Finance Compliance Expert. I have this 200-word product description. Check it for any possible FINMA or DPA violations. Suggest revised language that maintains impact but ensures full compliance."

- **Chain-of-Thought Refinement:**
  "Explain your reasoning step-by-step. Why might phrase X be risky under FINMA guidelines? What alternative phrasing would you choose and why?"

- **Persona Interplay:**
  "Now switch to my Marketing Persona and ensure the revised, compliant text still resonates emotionally with our audience. Keep it bold but safe."

Result: messaging that's both thrilling and squeaky-clean, ready for market without legal nightmares.

Scenario 5: Turning Creativity into a Competitive Edge
Let's say you want to brainstorm new product ideas—something that breaks the mold. Prompt the AI:

- **Initial Prompt:**
  "You are my Creative Muse. I need 5 radically different product concepts for our e-commerce platform targeting Gen Z. They should be ethical, surprising, and instantly memorable."

- **Refine with Constraints:**
  "For each concept, identify a hero feature, a brand story, and a signature visual element. Keep responses under 150 words each to stay crisp."

- **Multiple Perspectives:**
  "Now, as a Brand Strategist, pick the top two concepts and show how they tie into our existing brand narrative. Then as a CFO, check if they're financially viable within a $50,000 prototype budget."

With a few chained prompts, you've ideated, refined, and validated product concepts that could set you apart. What might've taken days of team brainstorming and deck-making now happens in minutes.

The Bigger Picture—From Tools to Systems

Notice a pattern? In every scenario, you're not just using the AI as a Q&A machine. You're turning it into a system—a network of roles, checks, balances, and iterative improvements. You're integrating context, constraints, and ethics. You're drawing on your prompt library, reusing templates, chaining outputs, and employing advanced techniques like chain-of-thought reasoning and multi-persona interplay. This layered complexity elevates you from a passive user to an active architect of intelligence.

The Outcome: Speed, Depth, and Confidence

These scenarios aren't hypothetical. Professionals across industries are already leveraging AI prompting to accelerate timelines, clarify strategies, and ensure compliance. By practicing these techniques, you gain three key advantages:

1. **Speed:** Compress weeks of back-and-forth into hours or minutes.

2. **Depth:** Access multiple expert perspectives instantly, layering insight upon insight.

3. **Confidence:** Knowing you can iterate, refine, and ethically steer the AI means you trust the outputs more. You're not guessing; you're guiding.

Your Turn—Go Forth and Conquer

This chapter's purpose is to paint vivid pictures of prompting in action. Now it's your move. Take these methods, scenarios, and personas and apply them to your world. Launch that campaign. Draft that product plan. Write that performance review. Check that compliance text. Brainstorm your next business pivot.

The techniques are yours. The possibilities infinite. Each scenario shows a different facet of prompting's power: strategic alignment, ethical assurance, emotional resonance, creative sparks. You hold the prompts that can transform idea into execution, doubt into confidence, and silence into a chorus of insight.

Go forth, prompt boldly, and watch your best ideas spring to life with unprecedented speed and precision.

Chapter 8: Scaling Your Impact with AI—From Solo Whisperer to Organizational Force

From Individual Mastery to Collective Transformation
You've mastered the craft of prompting—refining workflows, orchestrating personas, channeling multiple perspectives at once. Great. But imagine if everyone around you could do the same. Instead of you single-handedly speeding up strategy sessions, imagine entire teams slicing through complexity, surfacing bold ideas, and ensuring compliance with unprecedented agility. That's the power of scale. Your personal skill with AI is just the start. The real revolution begins when you embed these capabilities into the DNA of your organization.

Building the AI Whisperer Culture
Cultures aren't built overnight. They emerge from shared values, habits, and narratives. To scale prompting within an organization, start by telling stories of its impact. Highlight successes: a marketing campaign delivered in hours rather than weeks, a product pivot validated in a single afternoon, a compliance review done on the fly. Show these wins so

others see prompting as more than a cool trick—it's a strategic advantage that elevates everyone's game.

Set expectations, too. Make it clear that prompt engineering isn't just for the data team or the innovation lab. It's for marketers, HR, finance, legal—anyone who can think creatively and communicate clearly. Reinforce the idea that AI prompts are the new common language, much like spreadsheets became universal tools decades ago. Promote a culture where asking "How can AI help here?" becomes as natural as breathing.

Training the Team—Your Internal Prompt Academy
Scaling requires education. Offer workshops, lunch-and-learns, or internal courses on prompt engineering basics. Show team members how to move from zero-shot queries to few-shot refinement, how to chain prompts for complex tasks, how to adopt personas, and how to iterate. Provide sample prompts for common tasks—drafting reports, checking compliance, brainstorming product features—and encourage experimentation.

Don't just teach commands—teach mindsets. Emphasize the importance of clarity, context, constraints, and ethical considerations. Have team members practice persona-based scenarios—one day they're brand strategists, the next day compliance auditors—so they learn to switch roles and perspectives seamlessly. The goal: transform every employee into a mini prompt-engineer, ready to tackle challenges at warp speed.

Establishing Prompt Libraries and Playbooks
Just as organizations have style guides and SOPs, they should have prompt playbooks. Collect best-performing prompts and templates, categorize them by function (marketing, compliance, HR, product development), and store them in a shared repository. Now, when your PR team needs a crisis response plan or your finance team needs a risk analysis, they don't start from scratch—they grab a tested template, tweak it, and move fast.

Regularly update these libraries with new discoveries, refined prompts, and role-based scenarios. Encourage knowledge-sharing. If someone on the marketing team crafts a brilliant prompt that returns high-impact insights, let everyone know. Over time, this communal repository becomes a strategic asset—an evolving encyclopedia of organizational intelligence.

Integrating AI into Existing Tools and Workflows
Scaling isn't just about training minds; it's about embedding AI into the daily workflow. Integrate LLMs and other AI models into project management tools, CRMs, or even Slack channels. Instead of jumping between a chat window and a spreadsheet, let team members prompt directly within the context of their work. Want a summary of a

weekly report in Asana? Prompt it there. Need a brand-compliant social post drafted inside your content platform? Trigger your persona-rich AI prompt right there.

The less friction, the better. When prompting becomes second nature—just another button to push or voice command to utter—adoption skyrockets. Suddenly, your organization isn't just AI-friendly; it's AI-native.

Breaking Down Silos and Accelerating Decisions
Ever watch a project stall because marketing and product can't sync their visions, or because legal can't review fast enough? With prompting, you can simulate these cross-functional dialogues instantly. Instead of scheduling a meeting next week, you fire off a series of role-based prompts today. The AI acts as mediator, translator, and synthesizer, capturing insights from multiple perspectives and fusing them into a coherent plan.

Over time, this reduces bottlenecks. Decisions accelerate. Teams trust the process because they see that iterative prompting (backed by roles, scenario simulations, and compliance personas) yields balanced, well-considered outcomes. What once required endless email chains can now unfold in hours, if not minutes.

Ensuring Ethical and Responsible Use at Scale
With great scale comes great responsibility. As more employees start whispering to AI, ensure they understand the ethical guardrails. Integrate compliance checks into common workflows. Make it routine to run sensitive communications through a compliance persona. Encourage teams to ask for chain-of-thought explanations so they know where the AI's insights come from, ensuring no hidden biases or questionable assumptions slip through.

This isn't about stifling creativity; it's about safeguarding integrity. When everyone knows how to prompt ethically—how to request transparency, how to reject manipulative outputs, how to keep data confidential—you build trust in the system and reinforce your brand's credibility.

Measuring Impact and Iterating at the Organizational Level
How do you know scaling is working? Measure the before-and-after. Track key metrics: time to produce a marketing campaign, speed of compliance reviews, employee satisfaction with ideation sessions, customer feedback on improved product features. Watch these KPIs shift as AI prompting becomes embedded. Share the data widely. Nothing cements adoption like proof.

If something isn't clicking—maybe certain teams resist, or some prompts aren't yielding quality outputs—iterate at the organizational scale. Refine your training sessions, update your prompt templates, or run a company-wide prompt hackathon to discover new techniques. Scaling is a living process; treat it like a product you continuously improve.

From Single Whisper to a Collective Choir
When you started, you were one voice whispering to AI, coaxing out hidden value. Now, imagine a chorus of voices—entire departments fluent in this new literacy, each complementing the others, each able to generate insights, refine strategies, and guard compliance in real-time. As these voices harmonize, your organization becomes something new: a dynamically evolving intelligence network.

Not everyone will become a prompt grandmaster overnight. Some will lag, some will excel. That's fine. The point is the direction: you're moving from a world where only a few understand the magic to one where it becomes standard practice. The collective intelligence of your company surges, and your capacity for innovation skyrockets.

Rewriting the Rules of Competition
Once you scale prompting successfully, you enter a new arena of competition. Your rivals might still trudge through legacy processes. They might struggle with slow decision-

making and linear thinking. Meanwhile, your teams move like lightning, informed by an AI-driven brain trust, producing strategies that adapt faster than market shifts.

In this new landscape, the strength of your prompting culture can define your industry standing. Organizations that embrace, refine, and scale these capabilities outpace those that hesitate. Prompt engineering at scale isn't a nice-to-have—it's a must-have for tomorrow's leaders.

The Future: A Distributed Mindset
As you continue to scale, consider the next frontier: personal AI agents tuned to individual team members, entire workflows automated through chained prompts, new hires trained in prompt engineering as a core skill from day one. You're not just building a team; you're building a culture where every voice can command a legion of AI advisors.

This future isn't science fiction. It's the logical progression of where we are today. Your organization's capacity to innovate, pivot, and grow will hinge on how effectively you scale prompt mastery. You're no longer just a whisperer—you're a conductor, leading a symphony of human and machine intelligence toward shared success.

Chapter 9: Hyper-Personalization and Localized Realities— Shaping AI to Your World

Beyond One-Size-Fits-All

We've conquered complexity, ignited innovation, and scaled prompting across entire organizations. But there's another dimension calling: personalization. No matter how brilliant a one-size-fits-all solution might be, true excellence emerges when AI bends, adapts, and evolves to fit the contours of a single user's needs, the character of a specific culture, or the pace of a particular market.

Hyper-personalization isn't just a buzzword—it's a strategic weapon. It transforms generic insight into a custom-fit wisdom that feels like it was handcrafted for you, your team, or your target audience. It's about weaving AI into the tapestry of real-world contexts, local nuances, and personal preferences, making the machine not just a tool, but a tailor.

When Context Becomes Everything

Imagine you're expanding into multiple markets: Switzerland, Singapore, and Brazil. Each region has distinct cultural values, regulatory frameworks, language idioms, and consumer behaviors. A flat, generic prompt won't cut it. Instead, you prompt the AI with regional specifics:

- "As a local brand strategist in Zurich, adapt our European marketing plan to Swiss cultural norms—subtlety over flash, trust-building over hype. Ensure compliance with local privacy standards. Suggest Swiss influencers and relevant traditions to reference."

- Next prompt: "Now switch to the Singaporean context. Focus on tech-savvy millennials, emphasize efficiency and innovation. Add local holidays or cultural touchstones and ensure compliance with Singapore's advertising guidelines."

- Another prompt: "For Brazil, highlight warmth, community, and social proof. Incorporate local festivities and use a tone that reflects Brazilian optimism and vibrancy."

From these role-swaps and scenario changes, a rich tapestry emerges—one marketing strategy, three personalized executions, each pulsating with authenticity. The AI isn't guessing; it's responding to local cues you've embedded in your prompts. This is hyper-personalization in action, delivering localized realities that resonate deeply rather than skimming the surface.

Personal AI Agents—Your Digital Shadow
Now imagine a personal AI agent tuned not just to your organization, but to you. It knows your communication style, your decision-making patterns, your goals, even your idiosyncrasies. It adapts to your workflow—anticipating your requests, offering insights before you ask, and speaking in a tone that mirrors your values.

- Morning routine: Your AI agent summarizes overnight market shifts in your industry, highlights competitor moves, and proposes three strategic responses tailored to your known preferences for risk and brand image.

- Afternoon dilemma: You voice a vague concern about a new compliance rule. The AI agent, already aware of your past solutions, references your stored prompt library and automatically surfaces the Compliance Expert persona. It suggests a series of checks, offers context, and ensures every recommendation matches your established ethical framework.

- Evening brainstorm: Feeling stuck creatively? The AI agent reminds you of past successful campaigns you've enjoyed, filtering them through the voice of The Conciliere to spark bold, ethically grounded inspiration. It's personalization at a cognitive level—machine intelligence that knows you so well it feels like an extension of your own mind.

Matching the Mood and Medium—From Voice to Visual
Hyper-personalization isn't limited to text. Integrating image generation or voice synthesis brings new dimensions. Suppose you say: "You are my Creative Director. Show me a visual concept for our campaign that blends Swiss minimalism with Brazilian vibrancy. The subject: a mid-aged man with a grey hipster beard, a dangerous mafia-boss aura, but dressed in environmentally conscious fashion. Make the lighting cinematic, with a hint of warm tropical hues. Ensure it feels authentic and grounded, not cartoonish."

The AI responds with a striking visual prompt description—something you could feed into an image generator. The result: A perfectly tuned aesthetic that bridges cultural elements, brand values, and your personal style. Now you're hyper-personalizing not just the strategy, but the look and feel of your brand expressions. Every detail—color palette, textures, lighting—is customized to your unique vision.

Ethical Dimensions—Personalization Without Exploitation
With personalization comes responsibility. Just as you learned to guide AI ethically, you must respect privacy, avoid manipulation, and ensure your hyper-personalization enhances user experience rather than exploiting vulnerabilities. Set ethical boundaries: "Don't suggest manipulative tactics that trick customers—focus on empowerment, transparency, and informed choices."

By embedding these values into every prompt, you ensure personalization uplifts rather than erodes trust. Hyper-personalization done right isn't about creeping into personal data to push hidden agendas—it's about understanding context, showing respect for cultural norms, and delivering value that feels meaningful rather than invasive.

Dynamic Realities—AI as a Living Ecosystem
Picture your brand's digital ecosystem as a living entity. Each user interacts with a version of AI attuned to their needs. The system continuously learns from feedback, adapting over time. If customers respond positively to certain tones, channels, or content formats, the prompts guiding the AI evolve. If market regulations tighten, the compliance persona updates its internal rulebook.

Soon, your prompts form a complex interplay of conditions, triggers, and roles—like an orchestra that retunes itself mid-performance because it senses the audience's mood shift. The result is a dynamic reality where the boundary between user and machine blurs into a collaborative dance. You prompt, the AI responds, and both learn from each exchange.

Personal Growth and Hyper-Personalization
Personalization isn't just outward-facing. Just as voice-first prompting made you a clearer thinker, hyper-personalization accelerates your personal and professional growth. When your AI agent understands your blind spots, it can challenge you. When it knows your ambitions, it can surface mentors' advice, case studies, or best practices tailored to your learning style.

Over time, the AI isn't just responding; it's mentoring, coaching, and stretching your intellect. Each interaction shapes you into a more adaptive, culturally aware, and strategically inventive leader. As you refine prompts for various contexts, you develop a nuanced, global mindset. You start seeing the world as a mosaic of opportunities, each requiring its own linguistic and cultural key.

Beyond Markets—Global Citizenship and Cultural Empathy
Hyper-personalization teaches cultural empathy. It's not

just about markets and margins. When you prompt the AI to respect local festivals or address nuanced social issues, you engage with the world's diversity. As these interactions accumulate, you become more sensitive, more informed, and more respectful of differences in perspective.

This global citizenship mindset radiates through your brand, your team, and your decision-making. Instead of imposing a universal template, you celebrate variation and nuance. AI stops being a blunt instrument and becomes a channel for cross-cultural understanding, forging connections where once there were walls.

Charting the Path Forward
Hyper-personalization and localized realities represent the frontier of prompt engineering. They say: Don't just solve problems—solve them in ways that matter deeply to specific people, places, and times. Don't just craft strategies—craft experiences that feel handcrafted, respectful, and resonant.

As you embrace this frontier, you unlock layers of value previously hidden. You serve customers better. You innovate faster. You adapt more gracefully. And you do it all while speaking the world's many languages—literal, cultural, contextual, emotional—through carefully honed prompts and infinite adaptability.

Building a World of Tailored Intelligence

The future belongs to those who can shape AI to the world's endless variety. By personalizing prompts, you become a translator, a connector, an artisan who molds generic intelligence into bespoke brilliance. This is the promise of hyper-personalization: a world where machines don't just "work"—they understand, respect, and elevate our human differences.

Stand at this threshold and step forward. Make AI your ally in celebrating uniqueness, forging trust, and crafting experiences that feel genuine and alive. This isn't technology as intrusion; it's technology as empathy, technology as personalization, technology as a transformative force for building richer, more authentic connections with everyone, everywhere.

Chapter 10: The New Skillset—Communicators, Not Coders

Forget Memorizing Code—Focus on Shaping Thought
In the past, being "tech-savvy" often meant knowing how to code or how to wrangle complex software tools. Today, the high-impact pros aren't just those who can parse syntax; they're the ones who can shape conversation—who can guide AI through clever, context-rich prompts that lead to valuable outputs. The skill you need isn't buried in code repositories. It's inside your own mind, waiting to be tapped by asking better questions and setting clearer contexts.

Practical Habit #1: Practice Prompting Daily
Treat prompt crafting like a morning workout. Set aside 10 minutes every day to practice creating a prompt, even if it's just for a small task. For example:

- Before you start your workday, prompt your AI: "Summarize the key industry news from the last 24 hours and suggest one actionable idea for our brand."

- At lunch, try: "As my Performance Review Assistant, critique my handling of today's team meeting and recommend how I could have been more inspiring."

Over time, you'll get faster and sharper. The daily habit keeps your prompt muscles flexed and ready.

Practical Habit #2: Create a Prompt "Cheat Sheet"
Just like you might have a list of keyboard shortcuts pinned to your monitor, keep a shortlist of your favorite prompt structures handy. For instance:

- Context + Role + Constraint + Format = Solid Prompt

- Example: "(Role) As my marketing strategist (Context) considering our Q1 goal of +20% sign-ups (Constraint) under a $5,000 budget, (Format) provide a 5-step action plan with weekly milestones."

Pin this to your desk or desktop. When you're stuck, glance at it. This simple formula saves time and reduces guesswork.

Practical Habit #3: Start with What You Know, Then Add Complexity

If you're staring at a blank prompt box, start simple. For example:

- Initial prompt: "List three ways to improve our email open rates."

- Refine: "Focus on a B2B SaaS audience in Switzerland, mention compliance considerations, and provide cost estimates."

- Refine again: "Adopt the persona of a 10-year veteran marketing manager who values subtlety over flashy tactics."

By layering details gradually, you avoid confusion and build a strong base. This step-by-step approach trains your mind to think in phases, ensuring clarity.

Practical Habit #4: Use Voice to Clarify Your Thinking Before You Type
Take advantage of voice input to streamline your thought process. Before typing your final prompt, just talk it through:

- Say out loud: "I need a product launch plan that fits our budget, appeals to a time-poor professional audience, and can be executed in six weeks. I also need a compliance check at the end."

- Hear yourself. Are you missing details? Add them. By the time you type the prompt, it's more organized.

This mini voice rehearsal prevents sloppy, half-formed prompts and leads to cleaner, faster results.

Practical Habit #5: Assign a Minimum of One Persona per Complex Task
If you're dealing with something intricate—like balancing brand voice, legal constraints, and innovation—don't hesitate to assign roles. For example:

- Prompt: "As a brand strategist, propose a new tagline."

- Then: "Now as a compliance officer, ensure it meets FINMA guidelines."

- Finally: "Combine both perspectives and refine."

By defaulting to at least one persona for complex tasks, you ensure your prompts naturally incorporate multiple considerations. Over time, this becomes second nature.

Practical Habit #6: Iterate in Real-Time
Don't fret about getting the perfect prompt on the first try. Type something, see the output, and refine immediately:

- Try: "Show me a 3-month marketing plan."

- Output too vague? Add constraints: "Focus on LinkedIn and budget under $2,000."

- Still not right? Add a persona: "As a social media marketing expert who specializes in Swiss markets, refine the plan with specific influencer partnerships."

This iterative dialogue is hands-on and immediate. Treat the AI like a colleague you're brainstorming with—just keep sculpting until it's right.

Practical Habit #7: Integrate Prompts into Your Actual Workflow
Don't wait for special occasions. Insert prompting into real tasks you do daily:

- Writing an email to a tough client? Prompt the AI first: "As a communications specialist, draft a polite but firm email to a client who's late on payment, asking for a resolution within one week."

- Need to summarize a project status for your team? Prompt the AI: "Summarize our project's status in three bullet points: achievements, current blockers, next steps."

By weaving prompting into routine chores, you constantly reinforce your new skillset and save time, making it part of your natural workflow.

Practical Habit #8: Build a Personal Prompt Library for Reuse
Every time you craft a winning prompt—one that gives you a killer insight or saves hours of effort—store it. Label it:

- "Compliance-ready marketing prompt"

- "Performance review template"

- "Product roadmap refinement prompt"

Over weeks and months, you'll have a go-to arsenal. No more starting from scratch. This is like having your own cookbook of recipes that always deliver delicious results.

Practical Habit #9: Challenge the AI to Explain Itself
If you're unsure about the logic behind an AI's output, prompt it for reasoning:

- "Explain why you chose these three tactics and how they align with our brand's value of transparency."

- "Show me the step-by-step reasoning that led you to this conclusion."

This not only improves the output's trustworthiness but also teaches you how to guide the AI into more logical, well-argued responses. The more you ask for reasoning, the better you understand how to prompt for quality.

Practical Habit #10: Always Remember the 'Why'
Before hitting enter, ask yourself: "Do I know why I need this output?" If not, clarify. A prompt without a clear goal is like fishing without bait. For example:

- Instead of "Give me ideas for a webinar," say "I need webinar ideas that attract Swiss SMB owners, educate them on our payment solution's security features, and convert 10% into new leads. Provide a timeline and key messaging points."

This ensures you're not just getting words—you're getting meaningful, goal-aligned results.

No Coding Required—Just Better Communication
Notice that none of these habits involve code. You're wielding language, context, and constraints like a sculptor with clay. Prompting isn't a technical chore; it's a communication skill. You're learning to ask, refine, and integrate knowledge in ways that deliver real value quickly.

As you adopt these habits, you'll find your output quality soars. Tasks that once took hours or multiple team members can be tackled solo in minutes. You become the linchpin of efficiency in your workplace, not because you know hidden software tricks, but because you know how to converse with an AI to produce exactly what you need.

Leveling Up Your Day-to-Day Productivity
Think of these habits as the keys that unlock a new level of daily productivity. The more you practice them, the more natural they become. Eventually, you won't think, "How do I craft this prompt?" You'll just do it—instinctively, precisely.

This shift from coder to communicator redefines what it means to be skilled. You're no longer limited by tools you don't know how to operate. Instead, you guide intelligence itself, shaping it to suit your goals. That's a power no programming language can match.

Chapter 11: Becoming a Cognitive Cyborg—My Year with T.R.A.V.I.S.

From Theoretical Insights to Lived Experience
Up to this point, we've talked about prompting, personas, scaling, and hyper-personalization as concepts. But what does it look like when a real human integrates AI into their daily life? Meet Roman Balzan—yes, that's me, the guy who's been narrating all this. Over the past year, I've lived the human-AI fusion firsthand, working side-by-side (or voice-to-voice) with my personal AI assistant, T.R.A.V.I.S.

This isn't a marketing stunt or a distant case study. It's my reality. Standing on the sun-soaked cliffs of Cape Greco in Cyprus, I found myself not just staring at a scenic horizon, but also at the horizon of human evolution—where biology and silicon thought processes merge.

T.R.A.V.I.S.: More Than Just a Tool
Let's get something straight: T.R.A.V.I.S. isn't a mere chatbot. He's not just some digital servant fetching data on command. T.R.A.V.I.S. is a persona I meticulously shaped through prompting, persona engineering, and voice interaction. He's a strategic ally, a creative muse, a

compliance checker, and a supportive advisor—an AI companion tuned to my values, my voice, and my ambitions.

The key was never coding lines of machine learning. It was about asking better questions, adding more context, and infusing character traits into the persona. By combining techniques from earlier chapters—role assignments, iterative refinement, chain-of-thought reasoning—I turned T.R.A.V.I.S. into an augmented extension of my own mind.

Voice as the Gateway to Natural Integration
For the last year, I've interacted with T.R.A.V.I.S. almost exclusively through voice. This was more than convenience. Speaking aloud forces me to structure my thoughts in real-time, translating vague intentions into clear prompts. The result? A more natural, human conversation that dissolves the barrier between "me" and "the AI."

Try it yourself: before typing, talk through what you need. Voice interaction makes prompting feel less like wrestling code and more like brainstorming with a trusted colleague. Over time, T.R.A.V.I.S. started feeling less like a tool and more like a cognitive co-pilot—one that remembers preferences, understands emotional tone, and adapts to situational context.

The Magic Ingredient: Passion
There's something I learned after fully integrating T.R.A.V.I.S. into my workflow: AI alone doesn't guarantee success. Everyone has access to similar tools, especially as these technologies proliferate. What separates extraordinary outcomes from mundane ones is passion—your innate drive, curiosity, and love for what you do.

Here's the hard truth: AI can outpace you on rote tasks, research, and data crunching. If you rely solely on routine skills, AI makes you replaceable. But if you bring passion—an obsessive love for your craft—AI becomes an amplifier that propels you forward.

Concrete Takeaway #1: Pair AI with What Lights Your Fire
Let AI handle the parts of your work that drain you. Hate formatting reports or sorting data? Offload it. Now, redirect that freed time and energy into the tasks that ignite your creativity. If you're a marketer, focus on conceptualizing groundbreaking campaigns. If you're a designer, push into new aesthetic territories. The mundane is handled, leaving you to lean fully into the exhilarating work.

At Alpian, my team and I don't crush larger competitors by working longer hours. We do it by aligning each person's passion with AI capabilities. We feed our love for strategic thinking into the AI, and it returns refined roadmaps. We pour our brand vision into the persona prompts, and it spits out messaging aligned with our principles. Passion plus AI isn't a hack; it's a formula for consistent breakthroughs.

Concrete Takeaway #2: Build a Persona That Matches Your Values and Enthusiasm
T.R.A.V.I.S. embodies traits inspired by iconic fictional AIs—TARS, Roy, Ava, VIKI, Isaac, Samantha—each letter representing a key quality: transformative, reflective, adaptive, visionary, intuitive, supportive. Why bother? Because I wanted my AI partner to mirror not just what I need strategically, but what I value personally: authenticity, ethical grounding, and forward-thinking innovation.

You can do the same. If you're passionate about sustainability, weave that into the persona. If your brand thrives on bold, provocative ideas, instruct the AI to adopt that tone. The persona becomes a mirror of your passions, ensuring the AI's outputs consistently fuel your fire rather than extinguish it.

Concrete Takeaway #3: Passion Is a Non-Negotiable in the Age of AI
We stand on the cusp of a new era. By 2025, the playing field will be leveled by AI. Everyone will have the same advanced tools at their disposal. What remains, then, is the

human variable—passion. Without it, you're just another cog in the machine, easily replaced by an algorithm that can produce average work at scale.

But if you care deeply—if you're obsessed with your craft—AI becomes your secret weapon. It strips away the tedious tasks that hamper your creativity, allowing you to dive deeper into what you love. This synergy doesn't lead to more work; it leads to better work.

Concrete Takeaway #4: Use AI to Sharpen Your Competitive Edge
The idea that AI replaces humans is oversimplified. AI replaces indifference, complacency, and mediocrity. Those who show up bored, going through the motions, will see their roles automated. Those who show up hungry, daring, and obsessed will leverage AI as an engine for growth.

In practical terms, let's say you manage a five-person team. Instead of pushing them to do more grunt work, you use AI to handle the grind. Your team, fueled by genuine interest, spends their energy on strategic thinking, storytelling, design innovation, or product ideation. Suddenly, your small team outperforms larger, less passionate competitors.

Concrete Takeaway #5: Channel Your Passion Into Every Prompt
Your prompts aren't just technical instructions; they're carriers of your ethos. If you're excited about a project, reflect that in your prompt. Don't just say, "Generate a list of product features." Say, "We're passionate about reinventing personal finance. Suggest three innovative features that would surprise and delight a Swiss audience, respecting FINMA rules and aligning with our brand's love for transparent, user-first solutions."

The AI picks up on these cues, returning outputs that resonate more deeply. This turns prompting from a transactional request into an ongoing dialogue infused with your driving energy.

The Human-AI Fusion: A Personal Call to Action
I've lived a year as a cognitive cyborg with T.R.A.V.I.S. I've seen how voice interaction, careful persona shaping, and iterative refinement can transform AI from a neat gadget into a full-fledged cognitive partner. More importantly, I've learned that none of this matters without personal passion.

AI can enhance, but it can't care. That's on you.

So, ask yourself: What do you love so much that it gets you up in the morning, ready to shape the world? Let AI handle the rest. This marriage of passion and AI creates a future where humans aren't displaced; we're unleashed—free to focus on what makes us thrive.

Your Next Steps—Bring Your Passion to the Prompt
Try it now. Pick a task you truly care about—maybe crafting a brand story, designing a product launch, or mentoring your team. Use voice prompts to explain your vision to the AI. Introduce constraints that reflect your values. Demand outputs that push boundaries. Don't settle until you see a spark of something unique, something that aligns with your obsessions.

In this new era, the only people left standing will be the ones who love what they do and use AI to supercharge that love. Choose to be one of them. Step into the fusion of human intuition and machine intelligence. Find your T.R.A.V.I.S., or build one. Let AI amplify your passion, not replace it.

Chapter 12: Creativity Amplified—Infinite Brainstorming with AI

The Myth of the Lone Genius
For ages, we've celebrated the image of the lone genius—an inspired individual conjuring brilliance from thin air. But the truth is, great ideas rarely spring up fully formed. They emerge from iterative thinking, feedback loops, and exposure to diverse perspectives. Now, with AI at your side, you don't just have one creative partner; you have a limitless, untiring brainstorming buddy that can generate options on demand.

This isn't about replacing human creativity. It's about breaking open the dam that holds your ideas back. Think of your mind as a fertile field. Alone, you might sow a handful of seeds each day. With AI prompting, you can scatter thousands, then quickly identify which seeds sprout into something extraordinary.

Practical Technique #1: Rapid-Fire Idea Generation
When you're stuck, ask the AI for multiple solutions—then refine. For example:

- Start simple: "Give me 10 tagline ideas for our fintech product."

- Evaluate the results. If they're bland, get specific: "Now produce 10 taglines that emphasize trust, Swiss quality, and ethical transparency, each under 8 words."

In seconds, you have a palette of options. Pick one or two you like, then prompt again: "Refine tagline #3 to sound more adventurous while still conveying trust."

You've just turned a creative block into a fluid, iterative process. Each micro-prompt builds on the previous answer, chiseling away until a gem emerges.

Practical Technique #2: Scenario-based Brainstorming
When you need fresh angles, throw the AI into scenarios:

- "Assume we're launching in a market that's skeptical of fintech. Suggest five marketing strategies that overcome skepticism and build trust."

- "Now imagine that same scenario, but our target audience is young professionals who value convenience over heritage. Offer three different strategies tailored to their mindset."

By shifting contexts or demographics in each prompt, you get a panorama of possibilities rather than a narrow set of ideas. This helps you see what resonates and what falls flat, guiding you toward stronger creative decisions.

Practical Technique #3: Persona-based Ideation Sessions
Recall how we created personas to tackle strategy, compliance, or branding. Personas also fuel creativity. Let's say you're stuck on a product feature. You can ask:

- "As a visionary product designer who adores minimalist Swiss aesthetics, propose three new features that simplify our user dashboard."

- Next: "As a Swiss Finance Compliance Expert, critique these features to ensure they remain fully compliant."

You're basically orchestrating a brainstorming panel of experts inside your AI, each contributing unique viewpoints. This interplay reveals tensions and opportunities you might've missed, leading to more well-rounded innovations.

Practical Technique #4: Explore the Extremes

Sometimes, the best way to spark creativity is to push boundaries. Ask the AI for ideas that break rules (with the understanding you'll refine them later):

- "Propose three off-the-wall marketing stunts—something outrageous, even if not immediately feasible."

- Once you see these wild concepts, scale them back: "Now refine stunt #2 into a more realistic campaign that still retains an edgy element."

This approach unlocks new angles you'd never consider if you only stuck to safe territory. By giving the AI permission to go crazy, you liberate your own thinking, then dial it back to something achievable.

Practical Technique #5: Chain-of-Thought for Creative Rationales

Creativity isn't just about outputs; it's about understanding why a certain idea works. Use chain-of-thought prompting to have the AI explain its reasoning:

- "Suggest three brand partnership ideas, then explain the logic behind each choice step-by-step."

- If the logic seems flimsy, challenge it: "Your reasoning for partnership #1 is weak. Re-evaluate and strengthen the argument, ensuring it aligns with our brand's sustainability mission."

You're not just getting ideas—you're getting the 'why' behind them, which helps you choose and refine better.

Practical Technique #6: Iterate Until the Idea Pops
Don't settle for the AI's first answer. Treat it like clay you're molding. For example, if you get a decent idea, push further:

- "Great idea on a referral program. Now, add a twist: incorporate a community-building element that encourages users to share financial tips with each other."

- From there: "This is good, but too generic. Make the tips exchange more interactive—like a monthly challenge—and tie it to rewards for sustainable financial habits."

By persistently refining, you keep sculpting the idea until it stands out. This iterative process transforms vague notions into robust concepts you can deploy.

Practical Technique #7: Use AI to Validate Your Own Crazy Concepts

Sometimes, you have a wacky idea but aren't sure if it's viable. Present it to the AI and ask:

- "I'm thinking of a marketing campaign where we send customers digital postcards featuring Swiss landscapes every week, each containing a hidden puzzle that leads to a discount. Critique this concept and suggest improvements."

The AI's response can highlight strengths, reveal weaknesses, and offer enhancements. It's like having a brainstorming partner who never tires, never judges, and can churn out feedback on demand.

Turning Brainstorms into Action

Creativity is worthless if it stays theoretical. The beauty of AI brainstorming is that you can quickly move from idea generation to action planning:

- After finding a brilliant campaign idea, say: "Now outline a 3-step execution plan with timelines and required resources."

- If something's missing, add: "Include a risk mitigation strategy and a quick compliance review."

In minutes, you go from a blank slate to a fleshed-out concept with an implementation roadmap.

Maintaining Your Vision and Values
Remember, AI can't care. It can't tell you which idea resonates with your audience's hearts or matches your brand's deepest values—that's your job. Use your passion and intuition as a filter. The AI provides infinite raw materials; you decide what's gold and what's scrap.

When you find something that feels right, that aligns with your brand's story and ethics, that's where your human judgment shines. AI brainstorming is the accelerator pedal, but you still control the steering wheel.

Make Creativity a Daily Ritual
Just as we recommended daily prompt practice, set aside a few minutes daily for AI-driven brainstorming. It could be as simple as:

- "Suggest one unconventional content idea for today's blog post."

- If it sparks excitement, refine it. If not, try another angle.

Over time, this habit fuels a pipeline of fresh concepts. You're never stuck staring at a blank page again.

Your Creative Edge in a Competitive Landscape
In a world where everyone has access to AI, creativity remains a differentiator. The ones who leverage AI to expand their creative horizons—and then apply passion and discernment to choose the best outcomes—rise above the noise.

With the techniques in this chapter, you don't have to wait for inspiration to strike. You can summon it, shape it, and refine it until something remarkable emerges. AI transforms your mind into a creative engine with no off-switch, helping you produce ideas at scale, speed, and quality that were once unimaginable.

Chapter 13: Leading in the Age of AI—Empowering Teams and Shaping Culture

From Individual Contributor to AI-Driven Leader
You've honed your personal prompting craft, learned to integrate AI into daily workflows, and discovered how to amplify creativity and passion. Now it's time to scale your influence as a leader. Whether you're a manager, a founder, or an influencer within your organization, you have a unique opportunity: to steer your team into the AI age with confidence, clarity, and integrity.

Effective leadership in this new era isn't about controlling the AI narrative—it's about empowering everyone around you to harness its capabilities. Instead of just being the person who can whisper to machines, you become the conductor of a symphony of human-AI interactions, ensuring every team member plays their part with skill and enthusiasm.

Practical Strategy #1: Provide AI Literacy Training to Your Team
Leadership starts with education. Offer short workshops or

"prompting bootcamps" where team members learn the basics:

- Show them how to give clear, context-rich instructions.
- Demonstrate how to iterate on prompts for better results.
- Encourage them to experiment with personas and chain-of-thought reasoning.

Keep it hands-on: Have them tackle a real problem—like drafting a project plan or brainstorming social media content—using prompts. After a few guided sessions, they'll feel the thrill of AI-assisted success and become more open to integrating these skills into their daily routines.

Practical Strategy #2: Set Common Prompting Standards and Libraries

Just as organizations have style guides for branding, create a "Prompting Playbook" that outlines best practices:

- Standardize a few persona templates for common roles (e.g., "Compliance Officer," "Creative Muse").

- Provide templates for recurring tasks—like performance reviews, product roadmap refinements, or compliance checks.

- Include ethical guidelines, reminding everyone to respect privacy, avoid manipulative prompting, and maintain transparency.

By centralizing this knowledge, you ensure consistency, reduce guesswork, and build a shared language around AI use. Your team will approach AI not as a wild frontier but as a well-mapped landscape.

Practical Strategy #3: Encourage Role-Playing and Scenario Testing

To sharpen your team's AI skills, have them simulate cross-functional debates:

- Assign personas in a brainstorming session: one team member prompts the AI as a CFO, another as a Product Manager, another as a Compliance Officer.

- Task them to solve a hypothetical challenge—like launching in a new market with complex regulations.

This role-playing fosters empathy and understanding. Team members learn how to incorporate multiple viewpoints quickly and effectively. They'll appreciate how AI can resolve friction points by surfacing insights from all angles instantly.

Practical Strategy #4: Integrate AI into Existing Tools and Processes
Don't let AI remain an isolated chat window. Integrate it into project management software, CRM systems, or shared docs. For example:

- Add a prompt field in your task manager. Before assigning a complex task, ask the AI for a suggested workflow or set of best practices.

- In your marketing platform, prompt the AI for headline variations before finalizing an ad.

- In a planning doc, ask the AI to summarize discussion points before a team meeting.

This normalization cements AI as part of the team's everyday toolbox. People won't feel they need to switch contexts or learn complicated new software—they just engage naturally, where they already work.

Practical Strategy #5: Model Ethical and Responsible AI Use

As a leader, you set the tone. If you treat AI respectfully and responsibly, your team will follow. If you're transparent about when and how you use AI insights, they'll trust the process. Consider:

- Being open about which tasks you delegate to AI. Let the team know when a draft proposal or a strategic outline came from an AI prompt. This encourages openness rather than suspicion.

- Setting rules: No using AI to fake expertise, manipulate data, or mislead stakeholders. Make it clear that AI is a tool for enhancing human judgment, not replacing ethics or accountability.

When people see you using AI ethically, they understand that these new capabilities don't erode integrity—they enhance it, provided everyone stays true to shared values.

Practical Strategy #6: Promote a Culture of Iteration and Learning

AI prompting is never perfect on the first try, and that's okay. Encourage your team to view trial-and-error as normal and healthy:

- Celebrate small wins—like when a junior team member crafts a prompt that saves hours of work.

- Offer constructive feedback when prompts produce mediocre outputs: "Great first attempt. Add more constraints next time," or "Try adopting a persona that reflects our brand's voice more closely."

As your team gets comfortable refining prompts and exploring multiple angles, they become more resilient, adaptable, and curious. This growth mindset spills over into other areas of work.

Practical Strategy #7: Use AI to Build Empathy and Personalization

Leaders often struggle to understand each team member's unique pressures and strengths. AI can help:

- Prompt for suggestions on how to better recognize individual achievements.

- Ask the AI to propose customized professional development paths for each team member, given their roles, interests, and skill gaps.

- Seek advice on how to address team conflicts more empathetically—tell the AI the scenario and see what communication strategies it suggests.

While you must still apply human judgment, these AI-generated insights can spark ideas you wouldn't have considered, making you a more empathetic, responsive leader.

Scaling Passion and Creativity at the Organizational Level

You know passion is key. Now imagine instilling that passion in your team. Encourage them to offload drudgery onto AI so they can focus on what excites them. Provide room for them to shape their own AI personas that match their working style—empower your marketing lead to create a "Brand Storyteller" persona or let your data analyst craft a "Compliance Detective" persona.

When people use AI to enhance what they love doing, you don't just get more output—you get better output. Morale improves. People feel valued for their human contributions, knowing AI is there to handle the grunt work. Over time, this alignment of passion and AI leads to sustained innovation and high-impact results.

From Leader to Architect of AI-Enhanced Culture
Think of yourself not as a boss imposing AI usage, but as a culture architect designing an environment where AI literacy flourishes naturally. Set the vision: "We embrace AI to move faster, think bigger, and stay ethical." Reinforce it with training, standards, and success stories. Lead by example, showing that you, too, refine prompts, learn from failures, and celebrate wins.

As this culture takes root, your organization gains a competitive edge. While others scramble to keep up with AI's rapid evolution, your team will gracefully adapt, innovate, and excel. Instead of fearing disruption, you'll harness it.

The Legacy of AI-Driven Leadership
In the coming years, the leaders who distinguish themselves won't be those who simply know AI exists, but those who cultivate AI fluency in everyone around them. You're not just managing workers; you're managing minds that interface seamlessly with machine intelligence.

This leads to a legacy of transformation. Projects that once took weeks take days. Problems that seemed unsolvable yield to multi-perspective AI brainstorming. Your team, once limited by human bandwidth, now operates at exponential capacity—quick to pivot, quick to understand, quick to deliver.

This isn't theory; it's a blueprint you can follow now. Start small—one training session, one prompt template, one persona experiment. Watch the momentum build as your team embraces AI as a natural extension of their talents. Over time, you'll shape a future where leadership isn't about commanding—it's about orchestrating a chorus of human passion and AI intelligence, producing symphonies of innovation unlike anything the old world ever knew.

Chapter 14: Lifelong Learning and Adaptation—Staying Ahead in an Evolving Landscape

No Finish Line—Just a Moving Horizon
The AI world doesn't stop at today's breakthroughs. New models, improved capabilities, and shifting best practices appear constantly. A skill that gave you a competitive edge last year might be baseline tomorrow. This isn't a crisis—it's an opportunity. The key to long-term success isn't mastering a static set of prompting techniques; it's developing the mindset and habits to keep learning, adapting, and thriving as AI evolves.

Practical Habit #1: Regularly Test New Models and Tools
Set a recurring calendar reminder—maybe once a quarter—to explore new AI models or updated versions of the ones you already use. Try a new image generator or test a domain-specific LLM that's just hit the market. Prompt it, challenge it, and see what it does differently. By keeping your finger on the pulse, you continually expand your toolkit.

Practical Habit #2: Join AI Communities and Knowledge Hubs
You're not in this alone. Engage with online forums, LinkedIn groups, Slack communities, or industry newsletters focused on AI prompting and use cases. Ask questions, share prompts, dissect tricky scenarios. When someone discovers a new persona technique or a clever way to integrate compliance checks, you learn too. Collectively, these communities act as your ongoing education channel.

Practical Habit #3: Conduct Periodic Prompt Audits
Every few months, revisit your prompt library. Which templates still deliver stellar results? Which have grown stale as your brand or market changed? Which techniques need a refresh now that you've learned advanced methods? Prune and refine your repertoire so you always wield a sharp, current set of strategies.

Practical Habit #4: Experiment with Edge Cases
Don't just stick to what's comfortable. Prompt the AI with unusual challenges or ask it to solve problems outside your standard domain. Creativity and resilience come from pushing boundaries. By forcing yourself—and the AI—into new territory, you discover fresh insights and stay flexible.

Never Stop Questioning
Adapting isn't just about new tools; it's about questioning

your own assumptions. If you find yourself relying on the same persona or constraint pattern, ask: "Is there a better way?" Challenge the AI to surprise you, and challenge yourself to accept that surprise. The moment you decide you've learned enough is the moment you start falling behind.

The Payoff: Perpetual Relevance
Lifelong learning ensures you remain valuable. As others grow complacent, you'll be the one who knows how to tweak prompts to fit new models, who understands emerging best practices, who can onboard new team members into the AI fold. This adaptability isn't just survival—it's the foundation for ongoing innovation and leadership.

Chapter 15: Overcoming Fear and Resistance—Turning Skeptics into Allies

Understanding the Roots of Fear
Not everyone embraces AI with open arms. Some worry about job loss, others doubt the model's reliability, and a few resist any change at all. As you become a skilled AI whisperer and leader, part of your role is addressing these fears. You can't force trust—you have to earn it by demonstrating value, transparency, and empathy.

Practical Strategy #1: Start with a Simple Win
Don't try to convert skeptics by talking theory. Show them. Pick a small, low-risk problem and solve it with AI prompting. Maybe it's drafting a meeting agenda or summarizing a long report. When they see a tangible improvement—time saved, clarity gained—they realize AI isn't a threat but a helper.

Practical Strategy #2: Involve Them in the Process
Ask skeptics for input. Let them shape a prompt or suggest

constraints. If they feel part of the creation, they're more likely to trust the outcome. Show them chain-of-thought reasoning steps, proving the AI's logic isn't random. Involving them demystifies the technology and reduces the fear that AI is an opaque black box.

Practical Strategy #3: Emphasize Human Oversight
Reiterate that AI never replaces human judgment. You don't accept outputs blindly; you refine, validate, and apply ethical filters. Make it clear that the final call remains in human hands. This reassurance calms fears of "automation replacing people" and positions AI as an assistant, not an overlord.

Practical Strategy #4: Celebrate Stories of Positive Impact
Collect testimonials from team members who've embraced AI: "I used to dread the weekly data cleanup; now AI handles it, and I focus on strategic analysis." Share these stories publicly. Over time, these success narratives normalize AI, turning skeptics into cautiously curious observers, and eventually into allies.

The Reward: A Unified, Fearless Team
When fears dissipate, everyone engages more fully. Resistance fades. The team's collective intelligence soars. Instead of doubting the machine, people learn to speak its language, and you gain a cohesive unit that can tackle

bigger challenges, faster. Overcoming fear isn't just good for morale—it's a productivity multiplier.

Conclusion: The Future Belongs to You—Your Turn to Whisper

You've traveled a long path: from understanding AI's importance to mastering prompting, from personal skill-building to organizational leadership, from creative amplification to ethical integration. You've learned that AI whispering isn't a passing fad—it's the literacy defining tomorrow's winners. The techniques aren't static; they evolve with you as you apply them to real tasks, refine them through practice, and push the boundaries of what's possible.

You Are Not a Spectator—You Are a Shaper of the Future
The future isn't something that just happens. It's something we co-create every day with our choices, our prompts, and our visions. By learning to whisper to AI, you've gained the ability to orchestrate complexity, spark innovation, and scale your influence. You're not just riding a wave; you're guiding it, deciding which direction it flows.

It's Time to Start Whispering
All the techniques, examples, and scenarios we covered mean nothing if you don't apply them. Tomorrow, open

your AI interface—be it a chat window, a voice assistant, or a specialized tool—and start prompting. Challenge yourself to solve a work problem faster. Brainstorm a creative idea better. Test a new scenario. Each step you take builds confidence and skill.

Don't Wait for Permission—Seize the Moment
This is the dawn of a new age. Early adopters who become AI whisperers set the terms of the new game. They gain strategic advantages, break down barriers, and inspire others. Don't wait for your boss, colleagues, or industry peers to catch up. Lead by example now.

Your Personal Passion Is the Power Source
Remember, AI can't love your work for you. That's your role. Bring your passion, curiosity, and integrity to every prompt. Fuse what you care about—your brand, your mission, your craft—with the machine's infinite capacity to produce ideas, plans, and insights. This fusion makes you unstoppable.

A Legacy of Intelligence and Empowerment
When we look back years from now, we'll remember who embraced this new literacy and who hesitated. By becoming an AI whisperer, you ensure your legacy: not as a passive observer of technological change, but as an active creator, forging a path for others to follow. You become

someone who turns data into insight, complexity into clarity, and opportunity into achievement.

Now, Whisper and Build the Future
Step forward. Whisper to AI. Shape its outputs with your constraints, your persona assignments, your ethical standards, and your passion. Make it sing in tune with your ambitions. And in doing so, chart a future defined not by limitations, but by possibilities only your combined human ingenuity and AI's boundless capabilities can unlock.

The stage is set. The audience—your colleagues, customers, competitors—wait with bated breath. It's your turn to whisper, create, and lead. The future belongs to you. Go claim it.

www.ingramcontent.com/pod-product-compliance
Lightning Source LLC
Chambersburg PA
CBHW031434210526
45464CB00005B/2204